100 days, 100 GRAND

"**How to do Welfare**" first UK edition 2020

First published in Great Britain in 2020 by Redpump Ltd. Copyright © Chris Worth 2020.

The right of Chris Worth to be identified as the author of this work is asserted with all rights reserved.

This print perfect bound edition of "How to do Welfare" is **ISBN 978-1-912795-29-1**

See 100days100grand.com

"The conditional programmes inherently use poverty as a threat."

—Karl Widerquist, political philosopher

" *"Universal Basic Income is the only policy measure that will ensure protection for everyone, while giving the economy the fuel it needs."*

— Fuad Alakbarov, political activist

I lean libertarian. (Small 'l'.) A limited State, free-market capitalism, individual rights. Because that's the social system that creates economic opportunity.

Free markets, however, lead to something many people dislike: **income inequality**. In fact, inequality is sort of the point[1]. Companies compete because of the profit motive.

But wherever people compete, there are winners and losers. Richer and poorer. Haves and Have-Nots.

And when the Haves have what the Have-Nots feel is too large a slice, chaos ensues.

Most revolutions have income disparity at their

---

[1] The same is true of non-free markets, obvs. But that's a different book.

root. "The 1%" didn't start with modern Greece; it's been around since Homer starting humming. And mass unrest leads to violence and oppression. Which is *bad for business*. (Well, my business anyway.)

To salve this, we have welfare. But as practiced today welfare is a mess of special interests and system-gaming wrapped in red tape. So like others from all corners of the political map, I have a strange fascination with what might seem the most socialist policy imaginable: simply **giving people money**.

It turns out there *is* a better way to do welfare—one not about alleviating poverty, but enabling prosperity.

Let's put in some numbers.

CHRIS WORTH

THE MEANING OF POVERTY

The World Bank defines poverty as an absolute: US$1.90 a day. (About 700m people mostly in the hardscrabble global south.) Developed countries focus on *relative* poverty: households on less than 60% of median income. (That's 16m people in the UK— including twice as many children as pensioners.) Trendier today is "social exclusion": less worried about paying the rent, more about lack of ability to change their situation.

But however you measure it, it can strike quickly. 31% of Brits live payslip to payslip, as do 49% of Americans. Another 30% have to tighten their belts before payday twice or more each year. A quarter of UK workers are unable to save for a rainy day, with women hit harder than men. And in economic shocks like the Covid-19 pandemic of 2020, millions of people—not just the low-paid—lose livelihoods overnight.

Welfare claims to "get people out of poverty". In practice, it tends to keep the poor right where they are. Why? Because its narrative of "vulnerable people" assigns the poor a status they don't deserve: weak and helpless, incapable of forging their own destinies. (Which is false, as anyone who's seen an immigrant Mum fit three jobs between breakfast and the school bell knows.) While the votes in helping troubled communities—or, from some corners, vilifying them—have made "welfare" a politicised grab-bag of giveaways, each with its bewildering bureaucracy and impenetrable criteria.

The issue: if all you do is feed and house people at subsistence level, you're not solving the problem but prolonging it. (Perhaps for generations.) Maslow's Hierarchy of Needs (next) illustrates it best. If it's taking all your time just to put food on the table, levelling up from the bottom layer is damn hard.

That's why this book takes a different tack. Solving poverty shouldn't be about keeping people *alive*—the goal of most welfare—but enabling them to *thrive*.

Being told which forms to fill in, or which courses to sign up for, or what to eat, or where you can live, isn't the right way to do welfare. (Or *any* 'fare.)

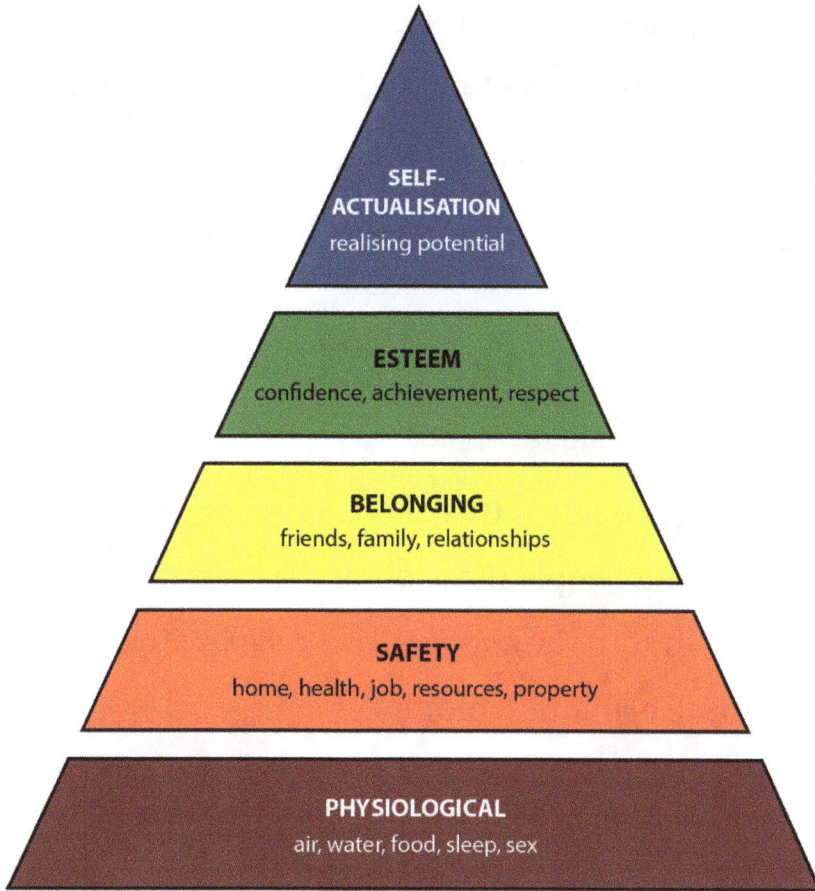

Figure 1: Maslow's Hierarchy of Needs

Which makes the what-success-looks-like[2] of any solution surprisingly obvious. It's about *opportunities*.

The opportunity to learn and train. To move where the jobs are. To plan for a brighter future. To *reach the next level*.

Because for most who experience it, poverty is that simple: *not having a choice*.

So the solution this little book lays out revolves around giving people more choices about their lives. Let's turn first to the *enabler* of choice in any functioning economy: **money.**

---

[2] "What does success look like?" should be the first question asked when starting any project, of any size, ever.

THE ROOT OF ALL GOOD

Money lets people take part in the economy. When you have money, you can make choices about where you live, what you eat, which products and services you prefer to spend it on.

Exercising these choices is how the economy prospers. Because they signal to businesses how to make a profit: supply things people want, at the prices they're prepared to pay.

That's all a market is: selling people what they want. There is no value in supplying *anything*—dried pasta, haircuts, jet engines—unless there's demand for those items from customers able to pay for them.

The positive here? In a market economy, the more money people have, the greater the incentive to sell them what they want, and the faster the economy grows.

And the greater the *number* of people with money, the more *customers* there are for those products and services, making the pie even bigger.

There's just no downside to having money.

So how does choice help people get it? One word: **productivity**.

CHOICES ENABLE PRODUCTIVITY

Macroeconomics is a big subject, but three basics cover most of it. Two of them (the short and long-term debt cycles) aren't under any individual's control. The third, however, is: **productivity**.

This matters. Because productivity growth—the rate of increase of people adding value in the economy—is ultimately responsible for GDP uplift, the wealth of nations, the difference between developed and not.

The productivity growth curve is the *only* factor that improves living standards over time.

At the personal level: the more capable you are of adding value in the market, the more employable you are. Because more people will value the products or services you provide, and the more opportunities you have to earn.

==But there's a chicken-and-egg here: the best way to earn more money is to have money to begin with.==

A cleaner working 60 hours a week doesn't have much opportunity to explore her inner software coder. Or lawyer. Or concert violinist.

Money gives the average worker the opportunity to find out how he/she can be most productive, and develop those skills to his or her best ability. (Yes, this is Riccardo's Law of Comparative Advantage, the basis of the magic of trade's "invisible hand". You're best *off* doing what you're best *at*.) Being productive leads to *more* money, and the next layer of Maslow's Hierarchy. But this multiplier effect depends on how much money you had to start with.

(Just for fun, imagine it as a mathematical function like $x \mapsto f(x)$. Poverty is solved by being productive, but being productive is a function of having choices, and choice is a function of having money.)

So there's one further nest to this function: your productivity is a function of the **skills** you discover and develop. Which is why the jobs most people in poverty strive at are low-skilled and low-paid. Because they have less money and fewer choices to start with.

So let's look next at **skills,** and how they can lead to that poverty-ending productivity.

PRODUCTIVITY COMES FROM SKILLS

Having skills makes you more productive, which is the route out of poverty. Trouble is, not enough people are gaining those skills.

The UK has a low skills base and poor productivity. Across vast swathes of the North and Southwest, jobs are scarce and prospects bleak; families whose ancestors mined coal and smelted steel have been in poverty for *generations*. As usual, the cries go up: Something Must Be Done.

So something is. Job training schemes. Means-targeted benefits. Grants and loans to sectors and industries the market has no use for, propping up old jobs in preference to creating new ones. In some regions of the UK government expenditure is over two-thirds of the economy. Needless to say, bureaucrats spending two of every three pounds doesn't make for a vibrant local business scene.

The issue: developing skills takes time and effort.

The UK organises skills into eight levels, from entry-level (mopping floors) to rocket scientist (CEOs with PhDs). Real benefits to productivity don't kick in until Level 4: skilled trades and undergrad degrees. That's *four years* after many people in poverty have to start whatever low-paid work is open to them.

(Note "low-paid" does not equal "easy". Few CEOs could handle six tables in a restaurant's busiest hour.)

So that's our virtuous circle to shoot for. Having

more money gives you more choices; greater choice lets you gain more skills; more skills make you more productive.

(No government needs to specify *which* skills; that's a decision people should make for themselves, based on their natural preferences and where they can add value in the market.)

And being productive gets you earning more and off the base layer of Maslow. When you've done that, you've solved poverty for yourself.

Now we've completed the circle—coming back to **money**, the root of all good—let's take a break and look at what welfare in the UK *costs*.

THE SIZE OF THE PROBLEM

Welfare is a growth industry.

The UK spends £265bn on welfare. France and Germany spend even more, at 25% and 31% of their GDP. The USA's programs total over a *trillion dollars*, despite few thinking of the US as a welfare state.

And despite public perception, relatively little of these sums go to wasters and scroungers. The stereotype of Moocher Kevin on his sofa watching Sky Sports all day is false.

In the UK, 80% of people on welfare work. Many full-time; many holding more than *one* job. While around a third of British households receive welfare of some sort, barely 15,000 families have been workless for two generations; of 26m households, just 2% have never worked, and most of these are aged under 25. Just £2bn of that £265bn expenditure goes on pure unemployment payments—fifty times less than on state pensions. Even among that tiny fraction of workless households, most people want to work. Earn more money, add to their skills, enjoy a life with more options.

In other words, most people are strivers, not skivers. Being productive is human nature; practically everyone *wants* to climb Maslow's Pyramid, and that's a Good Thing. (See "How to do Life" by the same author at Amazon for more on this.)

Government tries to encourage this, but large

bureaucracies without competition aren't good at enabling people to think and act for themselves. (Nor do they want it, really.) This makes welfare inefficient and expensive.

When you add in *other* social benefits available to all largely without choice—like healthcare and education—that £265bn figure jumps to £480bn. (Against total government outgoings of £772bn.)

That's a lot of money to spend on questionably successful attempts to keep people scraping by.

Which raises another question: is there a *better* way to spend it?

SIMPLER IS BETTER

Whatever that better way is, it needs to be *simple*. Because the moment an idea gets complicated, it takes on a life of its own. Interest groups square up, incentives get skewed, and opportunities to game the system abound.

In fact, that's an excellent description of how welfare operates today.

When the UK government increased support for Attention Deficit Disorder—making it the highest-paying benefit of its kind—Britain soon had the highest rate of diagnoses outside the USA. Because it was relatively easy to get a diagnosis, and profitable for the parent.

This is human nature. Any incentive that favours one group over another will attract people into that group. Welfare, as practiced today, is not *universal*: it's gameable by a swathe of special interests.

A second complicating factor is the *basis*. To someone starting from zero, providing calories and clothing will keep them alive, but not much more. Without opportunities, the recipient remains trapped. Like the difference between Minimum Wage and Living Wage, there's a gap between existing and living.

Third, most welfare isn't *income*. Housing benefits and food stamps don't give poor people much choice about where to live or what to eat; in fact, they're deliberately designed not to. Welfare needs to enable people to climb the ladder, not glue them to the bottom rung. That means giving choices about how to allocate those resources—which rarely happens with welfare.

Last—and most of all—deciding who gets welfare and what their needs are shouldn't be a gift of a public sector worker. The UK has 335,000 civil servants and over 3m employees on the public payroll, an incredible number basically engaged in Who Gets What.

(In one case, deciding a single mother's welfare involved *seventy-four* clipboard-wielding bureaucrats, an interaction costing over £250,000 a year. And you can be sure the mother didn't see much of that.)

Politicians and their functionaries shouldn't get to decide how different people benefit from the public purse. Particularly when they have a vested interest in making the power dynamic as lopsided and complicated as possible.

So there you have it: the problems of traditional welfare. Zero universality letting special interests take charge. A subsistence baseline keeping the poor in poverty. Inflexibility instead of income limiting choices. All adding up to the most toxic brew of any bureaucracy: **complexity**.

Fortunately, there is a simpler solution. And while it hasn't been tried in any detail, there's a wealth of data suggesting it would be a positive to both poverty and economic growth.

It's called **Universal Basic Income**, or UBI.

WHAT IS UBI?

==A Universal Basic Income is a fixed sum paid to== ==every adult citizen every month==. It's paid without conditions: free cash, for you to spend on whatever you want. It's *not* affected by what you earn elsewhere, whether you're a low earner, high flyer, or not working at all. UBI is *universal*.

UBI gives poor people a liveable baseline income that enables the choices that lead to a better life—and that doesn't get snatched back when they take a better-paid job. For those with more money, it's a welcome tax rebate that soothes ruinous life events like losing a job. (Of course, there's a question mark over how much it should be. Of which more later.)

The point is that universality brings simplicity. When *everyone* gets it, without shame or stigma, the special interests and system-gaming are neutralised and no vast bureaucracy is needed to administer it.

Sounds like nirvana? Perhaps.

Sounds expensive? Yes, it is. Very.

But welfare is *already* very pricey. And as you'll discover, the numbers make sense when you accept that UBI—the replacement for welfare—*isn't* welfare. Done correctly, it replaces more of society's costs than just that £265bn welfare bill.

Let's look closer at the welfare-rooted problems a UBI would solve.

1. The work-doesn't-pay problem

The first issue UBI solves is "better off on benefits".

In the UK, the maximum benefit a household can claim is £26,000: that's also around average household income. With the best will in the world, even a motivated individual will think twice before taking a job at £24,000 if it leaves him £2,000 worse off.

UBI doesn't do this. It's paid *irrespective of other income*, whether you're unemployed, taking a year out to study, or earning megabucks. With UBI, you're *always* better off. It's a bonus, not a benefit.

The main objection to this is that rich people get UBI too, despite not "needing" it. But this argument fails when you count how few are really "rich".

Someone on £100,000 a year—the top 1.5% of salaries—will still struggle to buy a London home. For her, UBI is a tax rebate—and a welcome one. The top 1% of UK taxpayers pay a *third* of all income tax. The top tenth, nearly *two-thirds*. And a top-percentile earner contributes £60,000 in income tax alone each year. £12,500 back is hardly a free ride.

The range follows that tried-and-tested statistical tool, the **Normal Distribution**. You see these everywhere in nature, from population dynamics to rainforest ecosystems. A lot of people in the middle . . . and not many at all at the top.

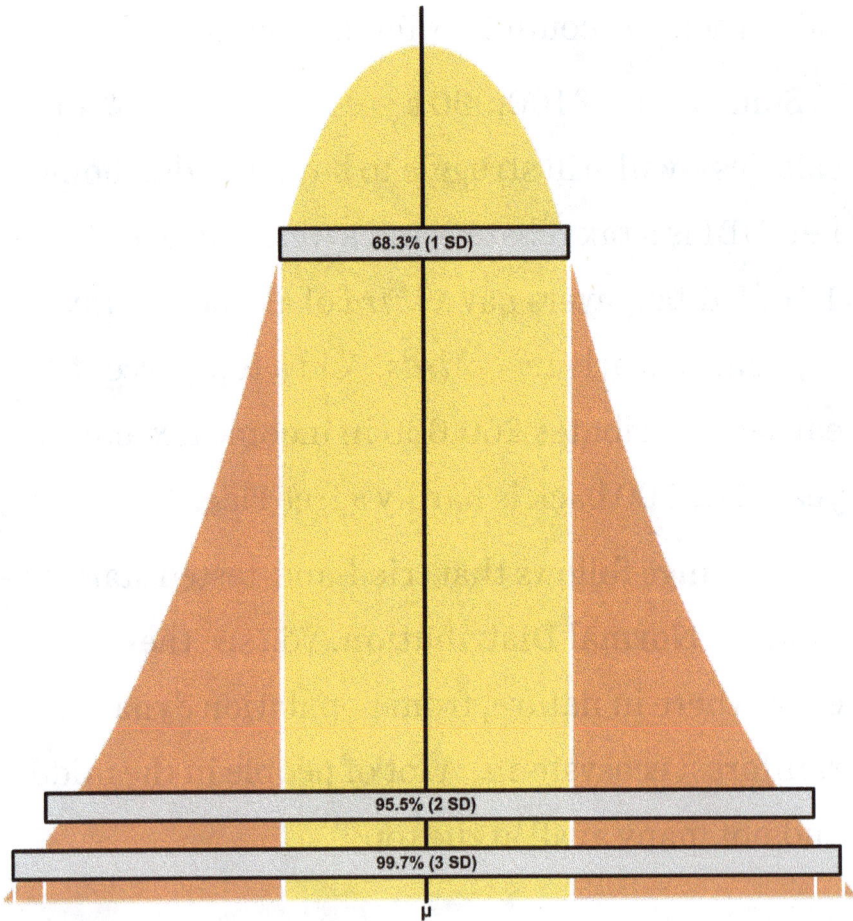

68.3% (1 SD)

95.5% (2 SD)

99.7% (3 SD)

μ

Figure 2: The Normal Distribution

A Normal Distribution divides a dataset according to how far each group deviates from the mean, known as "Standard Deviation" or SD.

The first SD is the yellow band: 68.3% of people, the majority of the population, fall within it. If you include the second SD, you've got nearly everyone covered, and they're all still fairly close to the average. Not many households fall outside that second SD: just four percent or so. (And that includes those who are very poor as well as those who are very rich.)

Translating this to reality puts the problem in perspective. Nearly 10m households in the UK already receive one or more forms of welfare, of a total 27m—a number that increases massively during economic shocks like the Covid-19 pandemic. In a normal year alone, public spending averages £10,000 per person; you have to reach the 84th percentile—those earning at least £46,000, the thin white line between the middle yellow bar and the orange one to its right—before you're paying *any* net tax.

Net net: if you're worried about the 1% freeloading, think instead of the 84% already doing it.

Only a tiny fraction at either side—the 2.25% who'll take advantage and loaf, and the 2.25% for whom it's more pocket money than lifeline—provide any negatives to a UBI, a number within statistical noise.

So yes, rich people get UBI too. But statistically, those rich people have probably been carrying you your entire life. They deserve a break too.

2. The means-testing problem

UBI is not means-tested. This carries a bigger bonus than fewer box-ticking bureaucrats cluttering up the country. It *stops welfare distorting the economy*.

All countries have regional variations in how expensive it is to live there, from property prices to the cost of groceries. Many jobs in the public sector pay extra to workers in these regions, like the "London weighting" of teachers in the capital.

Bureaucrats schooled in the welfare system might argue UBI needs weighting too, to be "fair". But big cities contain more opportunities. And taking advantage of them rightly carries costs. Those who want those opportunities should pay the price for them—and many do. (London's population continues to increase despite eye-popping rent.)

But in terms of UBI, weighting is just another form of means-testing. As are a thousand other attempts to deny market realities. Rent control. Price ceilings. Wage floors. And the whole point of UBI is to get rid of *all* means-testing; it's the feature that makes it work.

So: leave weighting to the open market, where employers offer higher salaries to attract the best workers. UBI, being universal, is not weighted for anyone, in any circumstances.

There's another bonus to avoiding means-testing, in all its nefarious forms: human dignity.

In welfare, someone who's just lost his job, homeless

and hungry, has to navigate a Kafkaesque corridor of forms and officials before any benefits are handed over. It's a depressing task for anyone. To someone actually *suffering* from depression, it's a killer.

This is what makes job loss a life-changing event, instead of the minor distraction it should be.

In fact, suicide is the third-biggest killer of adult males in many economies. And in half of all cases it's linked to the helplessness of not feeling in charge of one's own life. In other words, caused by the people who are supposed to be helping.

UBI brings back human dignity, giving choices and options to those who need them most. Which is, by itself, a great reason to adopt it.

3. The government-power problem

The social sciences have a discipline called Organisational Behaviour. Its guiding principle is that the motivations of the group—public sector agency, charitable enterprise, multinational corporation—aren't simply a scale-up of the people within it.

(Witness Britain's NHS: an inefficient, insatiable, insanely politicised coercive monopoly . . . staffed by some of the kindest souls you'll ever meet.)

The first tendency of the organisation is to protect its own existence and shut down any threats. Businesses want to grow. Charities continue jangling the can even after problems are solved. Bureaucracies tend to get bigger.

And welfare departments are no different.

With universality and no means-testing, UBI is very simple to administer. If you're a citizen, you get it. No questions, no forms to complete, and no criteria to satisfy.

That's Universal Basic Income. A refreshingly simple and honest idea whose time has come.

So next, let's look at a well-meant but destructive alternative many politicians focus on instead of UBI: Minimum Wage.

UBI AND MINIMUM WAGE

UBI sets a sensible floor on income. Because another economic policy—Minimum Wage—has the same goal, many people think UBI and MW are interchangeable.

They're about as far apart as you get.

Over 100 studies on the effects of MW have been done. None shows a clear positive, and 92% show a net *negative* effect on total pay taken home by the lowest earners. Hardly surprising, since Minimum Wage laws interrupt a basic truism of supply and demand: the price mechanism.

If Bob's customers want burgers at $10, but Bob has

to charge $15 because he's paying a high MW to his chef, it's Bye Bye, Bob's Biz. The higher the price of a low-value-add good or service—the kind most low-paid workers produce—the fewer of them will be demanded by customers.

You cannot be paid more than you produce in value.

In study after study—from Seattle to New York to Newcastle and Liverpool—raising the minimum wage decreased actual hours of employment offered. Meaning the higher the Minimum Wage goes, the fewer jobs remain for the lowest earners.

When two Berkeley economists set out to prove a high minimum wage had no negative effect on jobs or incomes in the USA, they ended up proving the

opposite. (Although they tried to spin it differently.)
Even when cherrypicking their data—choosing a set
that included only communities you'd expect to
benefit, i.e. the most deprived—their studies showed
that a 10% rise in MW correlated with a meagre 0.7-
0.9% decrease in the number of households in poverty.
In other words: even when two academics from a
deeply partisan institution (UC Berkeley is among the
most left-leaning colleges in the USA) got to choose
their anecdotes, the best they came up with was that a
huge cost to business (that 10% rise in labour costs)
leads to an outcome within statistical noise.

If we agree that most of the people needing help
deserve it—they're working stiffs, not feckless
failures—and that their main problem is not being

able to bring in enough money, you might think Minimum Wage would be a good idea. But all available data demonstrates it's not.

Minimum Wage is no substitute for UBI. In fact, a basic income negates the need for MW—and goes much further to boot.

So: UBI may be the answer. MW certainly isn't.

WHO GETS UBI?

The simple answer is "everyone". But this is one area where the simplest answer needs some qualifiers, in order to avoid negative second-order effects.

First, kids don't get a pocket money bonanza. UBI starts at legal adulthood: age 18.

While the UK's school system ends compulsory attendance at 16, many go on to vocational schools or further education to at least 18. Those who don't tend to end up in low-skilled, low-paid jobs without prospects. That's what this little book tries to *avoid*.

So a UBI that starts on your 18th birthday is an incentive to stay in education or training until that age or older, the level where productivity gains start to kick in.

But just as benefits tend to glue people to the same housing or town, reducing opportunities to move around for work, a badly-thought-out UBI would tend to restrict people's desire to see the world: to travel abroad, take jobs overseas, go where the opportunities are in a global economy.

Fortunately, there's a document that by definition minimises this: a **passport**.

Anyone with a valid passport is a verified citizen, uniquely identifiable, and able to travel. What's more, it's incredibly rare for one individual to have two from the same country. (Something not all that rare in the

National Insurance or "Unique" Taxpayer databases.) So UBI doesn't need yet another Big Government scheme to invade personal privacy further, like the ill-fated National Identification Card. The best criterion for claiming UK UBI exists already: a UK passport.

Political savant Dominic Cummings—the man who persuaded Britain to vote to leave the EU—sees a big objection to UBI coming from people who don't like immigration. So basing it on that soon-to-be-blue document ticks some political boxes, too.

Using a passport cancels that minus: it doesn't turn British UBI claimants into stay-at-homes. If you've got a passport and a UK bank account, you get UBI. Even if you're working, studying, or travelling overseas. Such people are often the movers and shakers of any economy; you don't want to exclude them from a universal benefit. Half a million young adults overseas at any one time, experiencing other cultures? Great. They've started life's journey well.

UK passport holder? You get UBI.

HOW MUCH WILL I GET?

Now the big question: **how much should UBI be?**

It's simpler than you think. And if executed, it simplifies the tax system further.

Most countries have tiered taxes. You pay nothing on the first chunk of your earnings, more on the second chunk, and even more at higher levels, all the way up. The **tax-free allowance**—the first part of earnings on which no income tax is charged—is a figure carefully worked out to burden the lowest earners as little as possible.

In the UK, this figure is £12,500. Enough for a very low earner to live on. Not in lounging luxury—but better than the State pension, and far better than Statutory Sick Pay or "Universal" (!) Credit.

In fact, £12,500 isn't far off a full-time job at Minimum Wage. (And of course, UBI doesn't stop you having that job, at any wage you can earn.)

So let's set Universal Basic Income at the tax-free allowance, £12,500 per adult, per year. UBI replaces that allowance: you now start paying tax from pound zero of your *earned* income.

This level enables the UBI Grand Plan: **opportunity**. Imagine an 18-year old, leaving school, from a poor background but rich in ambition. That teen can now go to university, obtain a Level 4 qualification or above, move across the country to a jobs-rich region . . .

whatever he/she wants. **Without** risk of starving on the streets.

Or a family hit by bad luck. Two adults losing their jobs as their twin daughters sit A-Levels.

That family's P45s are cushioned by a tax-free household income of £25,000. Maybe that's a big drop in lifestyle, maybe a small one, but with UBI, it's no longer disastrous.

They can take stock and plan, without having to take the first job that comes up. The girls, self-funding from those 18th birthdays coming up, can still go to university, or perhaps decide to work a year instead.

Maybe the parents will retrain, get *better* jobs. Or maybe they're close to retirement and decide to consume instead of produce from now on. (UBI is paid until death.) Whatever they decide, the family has *choices*. Without any frantic form-filling, bureaucratic box-ticking, or interviews with bored officials.

Best of all, UBI removes the *need* to retire. (Or to stay in work if the decades take their toll.) Artificial milestones like retirement at 68, around which a forest of complexity has sprouted with demographic change, simply go away. Continue working if you want to. If not, stop. UBI is a pension that starts at 18.

£12,500 a year, as a tax-free sum, in monthly instalments of just over a grand.

That's what you get.

UBI RISKS

Any big policy will have unexpected second-order effects. It's the main reason to keep them simple. And despite its simplicity, UBI will have them too.

How will UBI change society?

==The honest answer: nobody knows.==

Perhaps people will retire earlier, in the knowledge they've got a reasonable sum to live on no matter what. Or perhaps they'll work *longer*, a few days a week doing something that adds value because they've been able to engage in work they enjoy.

Wages for paid work may go down, with employers sneakily taking advantage of everyone enjoying a wage floor already. (Much as the USA's Wal-Mart runs sessions for staff on how to claim food stamps.) Or they might *rise*, since people have less incentive to take a low-paying job, and employers will have to pay more to attract them. Given the number of young Europeans working in Britain's hotels and restaurants who won't be around post-EU, UBI may even expose Brexit as the vindictive bit of racism it was.

Perhaps the UK's workforce will become lazy, sitting on its collective sofa enjoying the monthly £1,040 clicking into its bank account. Or perhaps it'll become the envy of primetime Germany and Japan: highly skilled and qualified with productivity skyrocketing.

We don't know. Because UBI has never been done. And given its nature, it can't be piloted small scale.

(Too many distorting externalities.)

So Britain's UBI scheme would have to be a 5-10 year all-or-nothing pilot, with some success criteria but no qualifying limits. With a sunset clause: if after this time it hasn't raised living standards by some amount, it ends and everything goes back to the way it was.

Everything has its price. And anything can fail.

The last word on this is that by any reasonable standard, existing welfare failed long ago. So if UBI fails, the country trying it hasn't lost much.

Child farming, aunt importing, and other system-gaming

If a passport carries a £12,500 income, it makes British citizenship attractive. Let's add one condition: you can't have a passport from anywhere *else*.

(Naturalised citizens, naturally, are fine. As are those who renounce any *other* passport. If you've got the papers, you're British, irrespective of race, colour, creed, or origin.)

Maybe some people might start importing distant relatives, or having extra children as a long-term bet on future family cashflow. But citizenship is a long process. And raising children an even longer one. It's fair to say this cost would be small.

PAYING FOR UBI

Obviously, UBI for all British passport holders (without a passport from anywhere else) is going to cost serious cash.

There are 46.4m British citizens over 18 in the UK. Around 3.7m overseas; call it 50m. So the total bill is £625bn. More than *double* the current welfare bill of £265bn. And total tax receipts were only £690bn.

At first glance, this throws UBI under a train. But remember: UBI is an *income*, not welfare. And income has economic benefits beyond government assistance.

So let's work out what it *really* costs, using the UK as an example. The answer is surprising.

1. Replacing other welfare

Easy targets first. ==UBI replaces all other welfare==. Housing benefit, Working Tax Credits, the State pension, unemployment benefits, Universal Credit, Statutory Sick Pay, Maternity Allowance, marriage allowances, everything. Because even among families receiving more than one of these, few rack up anything like the benefits cap of £26,000. And UBI adds up to £25,000 for a two-adult household.

This takes £265bn off our £625bn figure straightaway. We've already improved our cost calculation by nearly half, to £360bn. And we've barely started.

2. Replacing tax allowances

Next, recall that UBI replaces the taxable allowance: the first part of everyone's income before tax kicks in. With no tax allowance, the actual tax take from people's earnings goes up.

There are 30m earners in the UK. Even accounting for income tax alone, that's another sixty billion to pay for UBI, reducing its net cost to £300bn.

But UK tax includes other taxes: National Insurance, payable by both employees (the part you see on your payslip) and employers (the part you don't, because it's added to your gross income by your employer first.)

This swings in another bucketload of cash: about £1,500 in employee NI on the first £12,500 of your salary, and another £1,725 by your employer. (Yes, NI is huge.) Another £96bn in the pot, without any changes to the existing tax system. There are further benefits up the earnings scale, since higher tax rates effectively kick in earlier: another £7bn or so.

The net cost of UBI is down further, to £197bn. Less than the UK government has committed to various foreign wars, bank bailouts, or viral pandemics in a single year. And we've still got plenty of headroom.

3. Replacing public health

The National Health Service is Britain's State religion. Everyone loves it; everyone uses it; virtually nobody realises how expensive it is. (Not far off the equivalent of £5,000 per year per household.)

Another book (How to do Healthcare) outlines a plan for making the NHS a customer-focussed social enterprise rather than a cost-sucking monster. But in that system's absence, the NHS still costs the UK taxpayer £130bn a year.

But healthcare is a professional service, delivered by trained experts. Why not treat it as one, and make the part of it paid for by taxes from individuals (about 76%) a deductible on everyone's UBI, averaged out over the population?

Even assuming current funding levels, this works out to just £1,700 per year per adult. And let's be *really* conservative and say each adult contributes just *half* of his/her fair share. That's under £1,000, akin to the social insurance systems in France and Germany. UBI is still in five figures. And in all likelihood, public understanding of costs would bring this cost down. (Sunlight is the best disinfectant.)

This one very conservative action—remember, there's no hit to NHS funding here—swings another £49bn into UBI's favour. We're down to a net UBI cost of just £148bn. Up next: education.

4. Replacing public schools

The market distortions created by government schools are a major factor in poverty.

Richer parents can live close to good schools, whose children then have more life choices; poorer children go to schools on the wrong side of the tracks and stay there. The State sector spends £5,000 on each primary and £6,200 on each secondary pupil each year, an absurd cost base given its large class sizes and decrepit buildings. And *everyone* has to pay for these schools through taxes, whether they go public, private, homeschool, or don't have children at all.

This is why consumer choice needs to apply to schools as much as supermarkets. Because they should be subject to the same competitive pressures: ==innovate and improve, or shut your damn doors==.

So let's make schooling a parent's choice, paid for by vouchers deducted from their UBI payments. Once again, let's be conservative—and ask parents to contribute just *half* their fair share. Those who go private, or don't have kids, don't pay it. And the school system is still more than half funded by tax (once corporate and other taxes are taken in account) making space for special cases like orphans.

With UBI, such contributions are manageable even for a single-parent family—while Early Years, of course, become much more affordable. And a competitive market with parent choice would bring these costs down over time; plenty of private schools manage smaller classes and more contact hours for the same budgets. (Low-cost fee-paying schools serving the *poorest* pupils abound in Africa and Asia; parents pay because they value them above free government ones. The UK has made a start, with Academies.)

Education is a market like any other. So it should be competitive. When parents get to choose, schools will respond. And when the kids get to 18, those who want to go into further education have the means to do it, with £12,500 a year to finance their degree or vocational training in full.

At our conservative part-contribution, this takes another £70bn off UBI's cost. We're down to a net £78bn, with two twists to go.

5. Replacing administration

3m people work for Britain's public sector, with a total wage cost around £188bn. Most, of course, are not administering the welfare state. But 10% are. Call it another £18bn off our £78bn, reducing the net cost of UBI to just £60bn.

Of course, with the public sector headcount down, these 300,000 or so lost souls may find honest work in the private sector. Paying private sector taxes, rather than the merry-go-round of the public sector ones. (If a civil servant, paid for out of Treasury coffers, pays £10,000 back to it in tax, has it really gone anywhere?) The net effect is small. Call it £2bn off that £60bn.

But every little helps.

6. Economic expansion

A net cost of £58bn looks a lot better than £625bn. But at this point, even with the NHS and schools partly converted to the choice-driven services they should be, it looks like we're out of runway.

No free marketer could countenance £58bn in public expenditure with an honest heart.

Or could he?

As mentioned, economic growth is driven by demand, not supply. And in the first year of this UBI plan, the government puts £625bn into people's pockets. Net of the increased taxes they're paying on the first £12,500 of their salaries—the removed tax allowance—and their contributions to health and education now coming from UBI, call it half that in increased disposable income. About £300bn.

That £300bn is not quantitative easing. Not bank bailouts. Not military misadventures. It's actual cash going into the real economy of people buying and selling stuff to each other.

This figure doesn't so much answer the arguments against UBI as chop them into small bloody chunks.

What drives market economies like the USA and UK? **Consumer spending**. £1.34tn in the UK. Even if everyone only spends £2,000 of their UBI on what they choose, this increases to £1.46tn.

In other words, consumer demand has led to an

additional £119bn of goods and services richocheting around the economy. £119bn on which corporate taxes have been raised, VAT has been charged, people have been employed. ==Around a 5% GDP uplift==. Which *alone* covers that last £58bn of UBI cost. And more.

UBI is a pump-primer like no other because it's not directed government spending. It **allocates resources efficiently**, putting choice in the hands of the people. It's that "money upfront" that enables life choices, skills uplift, greater productivity, higher living standards. **All the good stuff.**

In subsequent years it gets even better. What happens when people make a habit of exercising choice, finding their purposes in life, learning and training and getting better at what they do? Salaries rise, living standards improve, the tax take goes up and the economy expands faster. It's a simple and virtuous circle government always wants, but goes to great lengths to complicate into absurdity.

This results in a lot more than we need to close a little £58bn rounding error.

The numbers for UBI add up.

HOW UBI SOLVES HOUSING

The Big Three of government policy are education, health, and housing. UBI gives the last of these an unexpected bonus: it removes any need for *social* housing, with all its scarcities, loopholes, and system-gaming costs.

Because the certainty of a £12,500 index-linked lifelong income for every adult is a *very* attractive mortgage proposition. Low-risk, because the income rolls in no matter what. Britain's competitive mortgage market already offers zero-deposit, low-interest mortgages to the creditworthy at five times their annual income; even for a couple without jobs, UBI lets banks offer financing for a £125,000 property (less than £1,000 a month) at no practical risk. Even if that couple only work for current minimum wage, their creditworthiness rises to £250,000+: more than the average house price in the UK.

And—as clever Singapore discovered, with its social housing that's mortgaged rather than rented—owning property gives people a proud stake in society.

==Look closer, and you'll find UBI is *packed* with opportunities like this.== Outcomes that increase life choices for millions, reduce government complexity, and do away with the need for vast bureaucracies of paper-pushing jobsworths.

So now the case is made for UBI, let's find out why nobody's ever done it.

WHY UBI HASN'T HAPPENED

Once you look at data, the case for UBI seems obvious. So **why hasn't it ever been done?**

Basic answer: because it's all or nothing. Which is a big risk for any politician.

The Speenhamland System in 18th-century England is often touted as the definitive UBI case study. It's anything but: limited to residents in a specific area, and paid on a sliding scale of need.

Later in 1968-1980, six US states piloted a "negative tax" which paid out a sum to compensate for a loss of benefits (the work-doesn't-pay problem) as recipients re-entered the jobs market. More recently

(2017) Finland carried out a small-scale experiment to pay a monthly £490 to 2,000 unemployed, but ended it when its government changed. Canada's state of Ontario also started one, but also cancelled it early.

The common denominator? Limited in scale and scope, **not one was universal**. All carved out a specific group eligible for the benefit. And whenever you give people of one status a benefit others don't have, it creates special interests with distorted incentives.

UBI opponents often brush this aside as a minor detail. In fact, it's the entire reason for each failure. If there's means-testing, it's not UBI; it's welfare.

Other wannabes abound. Spain has floated a "basic income" . . . for a subset of vulnerable households.

Stockton, CA is paying 100 residents a no-strings $500 . . . if they live in the "right" neighbourhoods. These efforts will all fail too, and for the same reason.

A second—and more cynical—argument is that governments have an interest in *not* doing it. Citizens making choices about their own lives and futures, instead of all-knowing civil servants doing it for them? Great heavens above! The lumpen proletariat might start *thinking* or something.

Combine these two arguments, and it comes back to a basic belief: **government knows best**. In centuries of public sector expansion into every area of your private life, most people no longer question it.

And that's the greatest barrier facing UBI.

THE TROUBLE WITH SOCIALISTS

UBI appeals to a broad spectrum. To libertarians, for the way it keeps government off the people's backs. To conservatives, for the way it keeps *people* off the *government's* back. To liberals, for its inclusivity and egalitarianism.

Strangely, it's often opposed from the corner you'd least expect: socialists. Why?

One word: **envy**.

Socialism, for all its fine words, is fundamentally a politics of envy: not about helping the people below, but sticking it to the people above. This envy of people better off has driven every populist revolution in history, despite the green-eyed monster provably impoverishing, starving, and outright murdering more people than any other politics, ever. (Around 200m since Marx picked up his pen.)

UBI sounds like the perfect socialist policy: empower the people by giving them the resources they need to live better lives. Trouble is, that's not really what socialism has ever been about. And anyway, what would they do afterwards, with nothing to complain about?

So in rolling out UBI, expect the socialists to be a roadblock. Even though they shouldn't be.

MOVING TO UBI

In *How to do Healthcare*, moving to a customer-focussed system was a years-long effort. Moving to UBI is different. We have to do it *all at once*.

In this book's example for the UK, it should be announced in an election manifesto with full disclosure and transparent numbers. It will be a big change; it will cost money in the first year; the chance of it raising living standards, while high, is *not* 100%.

UBI is a Big Bang. Which makes it fairly unlikely to happen the way it should.

But we've had Big Bangs before. In the utilities sector. In air travel. In financial services. All broke old monopolies and opened up vast new opportunities for the UK. And as the Brexit referendum showed, it's possible for big decisions to happen fast once the right third of the population gets excited about it.

In UBI's case, the "right" third is the low-waged. Those already on the poverty line, with household income below £18,000. Many of them working. All of them struggling.

To make UBI an electable pledge, you need 16m adults to think UBI is a good idea.

If any politicians are reading: this is a way to win the North of England, where low-paid work is concentrated. Or keep it if it's yours already.

16m isn't that many, right?

THE HONESTY OF UBI

Government's proper role is to protect your rights as an individual. It should not be in the business of, well, business. (Providing products and services.) Because unless you believe the Great Faker John Maynard Keynes (who owes his popularity in the public sector to his belief government deserved a big role in the economy) the public sector isn't *in* the market; it's an impediment *to* it.

The "right" government—small and focussed, with a strictly limited remit—would recognise this, and take actions that enabled maximum economic and social freedom. That's the only moral and proper purpose of government, and it's how government should be.

==But we're not going to get government like that.==

And if we're not going to get government like that, we may as well view our servitude to it as a plain and honest transaction.

I'll be your citizen—the means by which you exercise influence, execute policies, raise funds—if you pay me.

For all the freedoms it confers, UBI recognises government is your master, by making the transaction explicit: you're being paid to be a subject.

And if you don't like that, you can always refuse it. Hey, maybe being an outlaw could become a recognised life choice again.

BEYOND UBI: MOVING TO 15%

In the USA, taxes take an average 42% of all household income. In the UK, somewhat higher. In much of the EU, it's well over half.

Most people accept the social contract: those who earn pay taxes to help those who don't, those who are a bit richer pay a bit more. But when the average worker—not rich, not even prosperous—is forced to put *half his earnings* into the tax pot, something is wrong.

This is why the economies of Europe, with few exceptions, are sclerotically low-growth and unfriendly to free enterprise.

A doubling of gross average household income (the effect of UBI in a home with two adults) will supercharge the economy by an incremental 5% or more each year for the first few (let's say five) years. Once that's done, it's worth shooting for the next goal: reducing government expenditure to 15% of GDP. A sustainable sum for a low-cost government.

Why 15%? Because of a graph called the Laffer Curve, which explores what level of tax is the "right" level. (If tax is 100%, the economy contains no profit incentive so will not grow, and vice versa.)

It's usually used to work out the maximum tax a government can grab. But it has another use: discovering the level of tax with the *minimal* effect on economic activity.

If government expenditures are fixed at 15% of GDP, it turns out taxes aren't much of a drag on economic dynamism or personal freedom. So—given that government is still *needed*, to protect individual freedoms and operate police forces, courts and so on— the endgame of UBI is to enable enough economic dynamism to limit government budgets to 15% of GDP by law.

This is a bigger job than introducing UBI itself. But it's a complete transformation of the economy—a system that unleashes the superabundant opportunities of free markets, free enterprise, free minds and free people. So let's make it our longterm goal.

AFTERWORD: REVISITING MASLOW

UBI means everyone except the very impaired and the very unlucky can get off the lowest layer of Maslow's Pyramid, and start living a life of purpose and value.

This is how an individualist libertarian came round to the view that UBI is the answer. And Maslow backs it up further.

Unknown to most, Abraham Maslow added three more layers to his hierarchy late in life. Two involved cognitive and aesthetic needs: the urge for greater knowledge and beautiful things.

And a third—replacing self-actualisation at the

apex—was <mark>self-transcendence</mark>: where you feel a oneness with nature and society that goes beyond individual ambition, and expands to concerns for humanity as a whole.

Self-transcendence is the realisation that while the individual is key to any life-affirming philosophy, all individuals exist in a political economy, of people trading value and forming relationships. A **society**.

And a healthy and prosperous society –what UBI enables—is a worthy goal.

ABOUT CHRIS

 Chris Worth is a London-based copywriter and author of the guide to effective freelancing **100 Days, 100 Grand**. Google it or head for 100days100grand.com.

At work, he creates campaigns and content backed by meaningful insights, mostly for technology clients. (He does the research and analysis too, btw—his USP.)

Interests include adventure travel and extreme sports. He's lived in six countries, visited 60, and is a qualified sky *and* scuba diver with a passion for calisthenics and kettlebells. But he's never without his Kindle. See him at chrisdoescontent.com.